ASHOKA

ASHOKA WAS THE SON OF KING BINDUSARA WHO RULED INDIA FROM HIS CAPITAL OF PATALIPUTRA IN THE THIRD CENTURY B.C. HE EXCELLED HIS BROTHERS IN THE ART OF WAR. THEREFORE, WHEN A REBELLION BROKE OUT IN THE DISTANT PROVINCE OF TAXILA, HE WAS SENT TO SUPPRESS IT.

2

ASHOKA BACK IN THE CAPITAL. I DON'T LIKE IT.

ESPECIALLY WITH OUR OLD FATHER DEPENDING ON HIM.

I AM WORRIED ABOUT THE FUTURE OF MY KINGDOM.

YOU HAVE A HUNDRED AND ONE SONS, YOUR MAJESTY. YOU HAVE NO CAUSE FOR WORRY.

THAT IS EXACTLY WHAT WORRIES ME. ASHOKA IS RUTHLESS. HE MAY FIGHT WITH HIS BROTHERS FOR THE THRONE.

JUST THEN—

THERE IS A MESSENGER FROM UJJAINI, YOUR MAJESTY.

A REBELLION — THIS TIME IN UJJAINI.

SEND FOR ASHOKA.

LET'S CAMP HERE FOR A WHILE. REST THE HORSES.

A LITTLE LATER—

ASHOKA WAS CHARMED BY THE BEAUTY OF THE LEADER OF THE GROUP.

EXCUSE ME, LADY. TO WHICH TEMPLE ARE YOU GOING?

WE ARE ON OUR WAY TO THE CHAITYA. NOT TO A TEMPLE.

THEN YOU ARE BUDDHISTS.

YES!

COME ON, VIDISHA. IT IS GETTING LATE.

VIDISHA!

VIDISHA! A NAME AS LOVELY AS THIS PLACE. AND SUCH CHARMING EYES!

FIND OUT WHO HER PARENTS ARE. I WANT TO MEET THEM.

WHOSE PARENTS, SIR?

VIDISHA'S.

ASHOKA'S MESSENGER SOON RETURNED.

SIR! SHE IS THE DAUGHTER OF A REPUTED SHRESHTHI'S* FAMILY.

TELL THE SHRESHTHI! I WANT TO MEET HIM.

*MERCHANT

LATER—

SHRESHTHI, IF YOU PLEASE, I...

SIR, IS THERE ANYTHING YOU WANT ME TO DO FOR YOU?

I'VE NEVER SEEN OUR PRINCE HESITATE THUS.

I...YES. I WANT THE HAND OF YOUR DAUGHTER IN MARRIAGE.

I AM HONOURED, SIR.

AFTER A QUICK WEDDING, HE PROCEEDED TOWARDS UJJAINI ALONG WITH VIDISHA.

ASHOKA, A GREAT WARRIOR, IN NO TIME ROUTED THE REBELS.

THE REBELS LAID DOWN THEIR ARMS.

IN THE PALACE GARDENS LATER—

THIS IS AN OCCASION FOR REJOICING, VIDISHA. BUT YOU LOOK SAD.

I DISLIKE KILLING... EVEN IN BATTLES... ESPECIALLY BY YOU.

THAT'S SILLY. YOU SAY IT, BECAUSE YOU ARE A BUDDHIST, I AM NOT.

THE DIFFERENCES BETWEEN ASHOKA AND VIDISHA PERSISTED. MONTHS LATER, WHEN VIDISHA GAVE BIRTH TO A SON —

*MAHI =WORLD

TWO YEARS LATER, VIDISHA GAVE BIRTH TO A DAUGHTER.

LORD! THIS TIME, LET ME CHOOSE THE NAME.

AS YOU WISH.

I'LL NAME HER SANGHA-MITRA.

OH, NO! THAT'S A BUDDHIST NAME.

ONE DAY, A MESSENGER CAME FROM PATALIPUTRA.

HIS MAJESTY HAS NOT BEEN KEEPING GOOD HEALTH. PLEASE RETURN TO PATALIPUTRA IMMEDIATELY.

ASHOKA HAD HURRIED CONSULTATIONS WITH VIDISHA.

I HAVE RECEIVED A MESSAGE FROM THE CHIEF MINISTER. MY FATHER IS ILL. I HAVE TO RUSH TO PATALIPUTRA...

...AND YOU AREN'T YET FIT TO ACCOMPANY ME.

WILL YOU STAY AT VIDISHA-NAGAR WITH YOUR PARENTS? I'LL SEND FOR YOU LATER.

AS YOU WISH, MY LORD!

TOGETHER THEY TRAVELLED UPTO VIDISHA-NAGAR.

PRINCE! YOUR FATHER IS NO MORE. AND YOUR BROTHERS ARE FIGHTING AMONGST THEMSELVES FOR THE THRONE.

THE THRONE! IT IS MINE! I HAVE EARNED THE RIGHT TO IT.

ASHOKA FORGOT ALL ABOUT THE PROMISE HE HAD MADE TO VIDISHA.

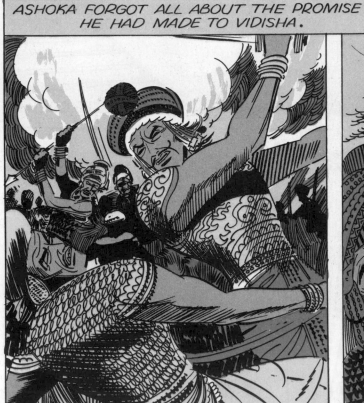

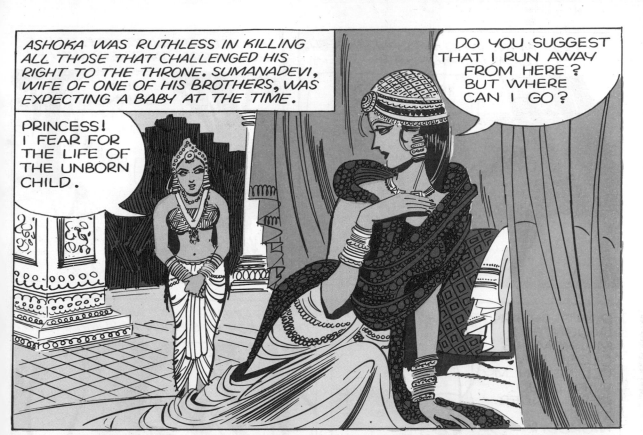

ASHOKA WAS RUTHLESS IN KILLING ALL THOSE THAT CHALLENGED HIS RIGHT TO THE THRONE. SUMANADEVI, WIFE OF ONE OF HIS BROTHERS, WAS EXPECTING A BABY AT THE TIME.

PRINCESS! I FEAR FOR THE LIFE OF THE UNBORN CHILD.

DO YOU SUGGEST THAT I RUN AWAY FROM HERE? BUT WHERE CAN I GO?

I CAN SHOW YOU A SECRET DOOR. YOU CAN ESCAPE INTO THE WOODS.

ESCAPING FROM THE PALACE, SUMANADEVI WANDERED IN THE FOREST.

AN OLD MAN, WHO WAS PASSING BY, TOOK PITY ON HER.

IF YOU COME WITH ME TO MY VILLAGE, I WILL ARRANGE FOR YOUR STAY.

SHE ACCOMPANIED HIM. WHILE THEY WERE ON THEIR WAY—

NO! I CANNOT WALK ANY FARTHER.

DON'T WORRY, DAUGHTER! MY HOME IS CLOSE BY. I'LL FETCH MY WIFE. YOU REST UNDER THIS NIGRODHA TREE.

IT WAS UNDER THAT NIGRODHA TREE THAT A BOY WAS BORN TO SUMANADEVI.

LET'S CALL HIM NIGRODHA KUMAR.

NIGRODHA KUMAR GREW UP IN THAT VILLAGE AND BECAME A MONK AT A VERY TENDER AGE.

MEANWHILE, ASHOKA HAD BECOME A POWERFUL KING. AT HIS COURT —

MINISTER, IS MY KINGDOM PEACEFUL? ARE THE BORDERS QUIET?

YES, YOUR MAJESTY. EVEN TAXILA AND UJJAINI ARE QUIET.

STILL WE SHOULD NOT REST TILL KALINGA IS CONQUERED.

WHY YOUR MAJESTY?

IT IS INDEPENDENT TODAY AND MAY RAISE ITS HEAD ANY MOMENT.

WAR IT WILL HAVE TO BE.

COMMANDER! PREPARE FOR THE BATTLE.

ASHOKA'S ARMY INVADED KALINGA.

THE SOLDIERS OF KALINGA FOUGHT BRAVELY.

AT LAST—

WE HAVE WON. KALINGA IS OURS.

I SHALL VISIT KALINGA.

AS HE PROCEEDED, HE SAW HORRIBLE SIGHTS.

HEAPS OF DEAD MEN! WE HAVE KILLED MANY.

OVER 1,00,000 MEN TO BE PRECISE, YOUR MAJESTY.

MERCY! WE BEG FOR MERCY!

WE HAVE CAPTURED 1,50,000 MEN, YOUR MAJESTY.

AS ASHOKA MOVED FARTHER—

IT LOOKS DESOLATE HERE.

LAKHS HAVE DIED, YOUR MAJESTY.

HE SAW THE SUFFERINGS OF THE PEOPLE.

OH! NO!

LET'S RETURN.

IN THE PALACE—

YOUR MAJESTY! AREN'T YOU WELL?

I HAVE LOST MY PEACE OF MIND.

TO ADD TO HIS GRIEF A MESSENGER CAME FROM VIDISHA-NAGAR.

YOUR MAJESTY! I HAVE BROUGHT THIS LETTER FROM VIDISHA DEVI.

WHERE IS VIDISHA?

SHE PLANS TO JOIN THE SANGHA OF BUDDHA.

ASHOKA DREW SOME COMFORT FROM THE PRESENCE OF HIS CHILDREN. BUT HE CONTINUED TO BROOD OVER THE KILLINGS.

ONE DAY, FROM HIS PALACE WINDOW, HE SAW A MONK PASSING ALONG THE ROAD.

WHO CAN THIS BE? WHY DO I FEEL DRAWN TOWARDS HIM?

GO! QUICK! REQUEST THAT MONK TO COME HERE.

WHEN THE MONK CAME —

VENERABLE ONE, WHO ARE YOU?

DON'T YOU SEE, WHO I AM? A BUDDHIST MONK.

MAY I KNOW YOUR NAME, PLEASE?

MY MOTHER CALLED ME NIGRODHA KUMAR.

NIGRODHA KUMAR! I KNOW, THAT IS THE NAME OF MY BROTHER'S SON.

YES. I AM YOUR NEPHEW. I CAN GUESS WHAT IS GOING ON IN YOUR MIND.

A TRANSFORMATION CAME ABOUT IN ASHOKA. ALL HIS ATTENTION NOW WAS ON BRINGING PEACE AND HAPPINESS TO THE PEOPLE.

FOR THE COMFORT OF TRAVELLERS, EVEN IN THE WOODS, HE BUILT REST HOUSES AND DISPENSARIES.

HE ERECTED PILLARS...

...AND CARVED INSTRUCTIONS ON ROCKS.

देवान प्रिये
पियदसि लाजा
हेव आहा जाा.

PRIYADARSHI, THE BELOVED KING OF GOD SAYS THIS ---

ONE DAY —

I HAVE GIVEN AWAY ALL THINGS DEAR TO ME.

EXCEPT...

EXCEPT WHAT, MAHINDRA?

YOUR CHILDREN.

YOUR SON WISHES TO JOIN THE SANGHA.

MUST YOU, MAHINDRA? IT IS WITH A HEAVY HEART — BUT I GIVE YOU PERMISSION.

FATHER, ALLOW ME TO JOIN THE NUNNERY.

OH! SANGHAMITRA!!

DO NOT GRIEVE.

BY SACRIFICING YOUR DEAR ONES YOU HAVE PROVED THAT DHARMA IS DEAR TO YOU. YOU ARE INDEED, DHARMASHOKA.

THUS ASHOKA BECAME DHARMASHOKA. HE RULED FOR MANY YEARS AND LOOKED AFTER THE WELFARE OF THE SUBJECTS OF HIS VAST EMPIRE AS A FATHER WOULD LOOK AFTER HIS CHILDREN.

THE FIVE PRINCIPLES OF CO-EXISTENCE, WHICH HE PROPA-GATED, ARE STILL RESPECTED THE WORLD OVER. THE ASHOKA PILLAR AT SARNATH REMINDS US EVEN TILL THIS DAY OF HIS GREATNESS. THE 'DHARMA CHAKRA' ON THE ASHOKA PILLAR ADORNS OUR NATIONAL FLAG.

SAMUDRA GUPTA

THE LUTE-PLAYING CONQUEROR

The route to your roots

SAMUDRA GUPTA

Can a music-loving, scholarly prince be a successful king? Will a skilled and committed warrior encourage the arts and science? Samudra Gupta proved he was a multi-faceted ruler. By bringing peace to a huge area of the warring subcontinent, this benevolent king gave his people the leisure to be creative. His court official Harishena engraved his master's achievement on the Ashoka pillar in Allahabad.

Script
Kamala Chandrakant

Illustrations
Souren Roy

Editor
Anant Pai

Cover illustration by: Ramesh Umrotkar

THE EARLY DECADES OF THE FOURTH CENTURY: THE SONS OF THE KING AND THE MINISTERS OF ANCIENT MAGADHA WERE LISTENING WITH RAPT ATTENTION TO THEIR GURU WHEN...

...CHANDRA GUPTA, THE KING OF MAGADHA, SILENTLY RODE UP, DISMOUNTED...

...AND HID HIMSELF BEHIND A BUSH.

YOU MAY NOW CHOOSE YOUR WEAPONS AND YOUR OPPONENTS.

THE KING OBSERVED HIS ELDEST SON, KACHA, WITH PRIDE.

SURELY, NONE CAN WIELD THE SWORD AS DEFTLY AS HE DOES!

BUT AS KACHA WARMED UP...

...CHANDRA GUPTA GREW ALARMED.

HE'S LOST CONTROL OF HIM-SELF! HE'LL KILL HARISHENA!

THE GURU HOWEVER WAS ALERT.

KACHA!

KACHA IS AN EXCELLENT SWORDSMAN. BUT...

HE IS YOUR ENEMY, SAMUDRA GUPTA. FIGHT HIM. SHOW SOME SPIRIT.

OH! OH! HIS OPPONENT HAS GOT THE BETTER OF HIM.

COME ON, SAMUDRA GUPTA! FIGHT!

THAT'S IT! THAT WAS EXCELLENT!

SUDDENLY SAMUDRA GUPTA FLUNG HIS AXE ASIDE ...

... AND EMBRACED HIS OPPONENT.

SOON —

WELL DONE, MY SON. I AM PROUD OF YOUR SKILL... YOUR SELF-CONTROL... AND MOST OF ALL...

MAHARAJ!

FATHER!

... I AM PROUD OF THE WAY YOU TREATED YOUR LOSING OPPONENT!

LATER, AS THEY WALKED TOWARDS THE HALL WHERE MUSIC WAS TAUGHT —

WHY MUST A KSHATRIYA FIGHT?

FOR FAME! FOR GLORY!

A KSHATRIYA WHO FIGHTS FOR PERSONAL GLORY ONLY BRINGS MISERY IN HIS WAKE.

BLOODSHED, DESTRUCTION, POVERTY, INSECURITY... THESE FOLLOW WANTON WARFARE.

HA! HA! HA! FINE-SOUNDING WORDS, BUT ABSOLUTELY SENSELESS.

SAMUDRA GUPTA, DO YOU REALLY BELIEVE THAT A KSHATRIYA MUST NOT FIGHT?

OH, HE MUST! BUT NOT FOR PERSONAL GLORY.

HE MUST FIGHT FOR ORDER... FOR STABILITY. HE MUST FIGHT TO UPHOLD DHARMA... LIKE THE PANDAVAS.

5

THE PANDAVAS, HE SAYS. WHAT A FINE EXAMPLE! KSHATRIYAS WHO FOUGHT DRONA AND BHEESHMA, THEIR GURUS!

WHOM THEY DEEPLY RESPECT-ED, LET ME REMIND YOU.

BUT DRONA AND BHEESHMA HAD TO BE FOUGHT AS THEY WERE IN THE ENEMY CAMP.

AN ENEMY CAMP OF BLOOD RELATIVES! PAH! GIVE UP, SAMUDRA GUPTA.

THE ONLY RELATIVE A KSHATRIYA HAS IS DHARMA.

AND HE MUST BE PREPARED TO FIGHT EVEN HIS OWN BROTHER IN DEFENCE OF DHARMA.

VERY TRUE, MY SON.

MAHARAJ!

HE IS RIGHT, KACHA. ONLY THOSE WHO ARE CAPABLE OF PROTECTING DHARMA CAN CLAIM THE RIGHT TO KINGSHIP. AND THE KAURAVAS HAD BY THEIR IGNOBLE ACTIONS LOST THAT RIGHT.

INSIDE THE MUSIC HALL —

IN THIS DISCIPLINE SAMUDRA GUPTA EXCELS ALL. HARISHENA IS GOOD AT COMPOSING VERSES BUT SAMUDRA GUPTA OUTSHINES HIM IN RENDERING THEM.

HARISHENA, HAVE YOU COMPOSED THE VERSES?

YES, SIR.

HARISHENA RECITED THE LYRIC, THE GURU COMPOSED THE MUSIC AND —

ALL RIGHT. LET'S BEGIN. SA-A-A-A

WHEN I BECOME KING, I WILL SPARE MY SONS THIS SILLY ROUTINE.

KACHA DID NOT KNOW THAT HE WAS BEING OBSERVED.

THEY WILL LEARN TO FIGHT AND CONQUER... NOT INDULGE IN SUCH FUTILE PURSUITS.

SIR, I...I WOULD LIKE TO PLAY A PIECE THAT WAS NOT TAUGHT HERE. I WANT TO KNOW WHAT YOU THINK OF IT.

PLAY IT SON, BY ALL MEANS DO!

WHEN THE PIECE WAS OVER —

DELIGHTFUL! WHO COMPOSED THE LYRIC? WHO SET THE MUSIC?

MY EFFORT, SIR. BOTH, THE LYRIC AND THE MUSIC.

WHY, YOU HAVE PUT TO SHAME BOTH TUMBURU AND NARADA!

YOU SHOULD HAVE BEEN THE SON OF A POET OR A MUSICIAN...

...NOT A KING!

PERHAPS, YES. FOR...

...WITHOUT MUSIC, MY SOUL, THE SOUL OF A PEOPLE WOULD PERISH.

THEN WHY DO YOU PRACTISE THE MILITARY ARTS?

BECAUSE THE BEAUTIFUL PURSUITS OF PEACE CAN FLOURISH ONLY WHEN A KINGDOM IS FREE FROM WARS AND WANT.

AND AS THE SON OF A KING ONE OF MY DUTIES IS TO HELP THE KING IN ENSURING PEACE FOR THE FINER PURSUITS.

NONSENSE!

THE TRUE KING DOES NOT STOP FIGHTING AND ANNEXING TERRITORIES FOR GREATER POWER.

MAHARAJ, AS YOUR ELDEST SON AND HEIR TO THE THRONE MY HANDS ARE MEANT TO WIELD THE SWORD...NOT PLAY THE LUTE!

HM-M-M!

THE BOYS ARE FEARLESS, STRONG AND INTELLIGENT.

AND YET EACH ONE IS SO DIFFERENT...

CHANDRA GUPTA THEN LEFT FOR HIS PALACE.

THERE, KUMARADEVI, THE LICHCHAVI PRINCESS WHO WAS HIS FAVOURITE QUEEN AND THE MOTHER OF SAMUDRA GUPTA, WELCOMED HIM WITH A SMILE.

HAVE YOU FOUND THE ANSWER TO YOUR QUESTION?

YES. I THINK I HAVE.

BUT WHY DID YOU WANT TO KNOW WHICH OF YOUR SONS WAS THE BEST?

BECAUSE HE...

... IS GOING TO BE MY SUCCESSOR!

I...I DON'T UNDERSTAND.

ACCORDING TO TRADITION, YOUR ELDEST SON IS YOUR SUCCESSOR.

YE-ES. BUT...

...TRADITION WILL HAVE TO BE WAIVED IN THIS CASE.

OH!

10

MY SUCCESSOR HAS GREAT TASKS AHEAD OF HIM... A GREAT FUTURE.

KUMARADEVI, OUR MARRIAGE BROUGHT STRENGTH AND PEACE TO THE KINGDOM.

ANY OF MY SONS CAN WIN WARS AND EXPAND THE KINGDOM.

BUT ONLY ONE WHO HAS MASTERED THE ARTS OF PEACE AS WELL CAN BRING LIFE AND GLORY TO IT.

11

WHEN IT WAS TIME FOR HIS SONS TO GET MARRIED, CHANDRA GUPTA RESERVED THE MOST ACCOMPLISHED BRIDE FOR SAMUDRA GUPTA.

SHOULDN'T THE BEST ALLIANCE GO TO YOUR ELDEST SON?

NO. SAMUDRA GUPTA WILL MARRY DATTADEVI AND FOR VERY GOOD REASONS.

AND SO SAMUDRA GUPTA WAS MARRIED TO DATTADEVI +

ONE DAY WHILE CHANDRA GUPTA, HIS SONS AND HIS RETINUE WERE OUT ON A HUNT —

HE HASN'T SEEN THAT TIGER!

AS THE TIGER SPRANG...

+ DATTADEVI LATER BECAME THE MOTHER OF CHANDRA GUPTA II.

...A SPEAR BROUGHT IT ROARING TO THE GROUND.

SOMEONE IN OUR PARTY HAS BEEN VERY ALERT!

CHANDRA GUPTA PRETENDED TO BE ANGRY.

WHO SENT THAT SPEAR AND DENIED ME THE PRIVILEGE OF DEFENDING MYSELF?

IT WAS SAMUDRA GUPTA, FATHER.

I SHOULD HAVE KNOWN!

YOU HAVE BEEN PRESUMPTUOUS.

IGNORING KACHA'S COMMENT, SAMUDRA GUPTA ADDRESSED HIS FATHER.

I...I DID NOT MEAN TO BE AUDACIOUS, FATHER. I WAS PROTECTING THE LIFE OF MY KING.

YOU HAD NOT SEEN THE BEAST. IT COULD HAVE KILLED YOU.

THAT WAS A NARROW ESCAPE. I MUST DO WHAT I HAVE DECIDED TO DO, WITHOUT DELAY.

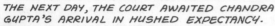

THE NEXT DAY, THE COURT AWAITED CHANDRA GUPTA'S ARRIVAL IN HUSHED EXPECTANCY.

WHY HAS HE CALLED THIS SPECIAL COURT?

IT MUST BE TO DISCUSS THE PLANS OF SOME CAMPAIGN.

OUR KING HAS NEVER FAVOURED A POLICY OF AGGRESSION AND EXPANSION.

THEN WHAT COULD IT BE?

THE ARRIVAL OF THE KING, HIS FAVOURITE QUEEN AND THE PRINCES PUT AN END TO THE SPECULATION.

WHEN ALL WERE SEATED —

WHAT YOU ARE ABOUT TO WITNESS TODAY MAY AMAZE SOME... DISAPPOINT A FEW... AND PLEASE MANY.

BUT WHAT I PROPOSE TO DO IS BEING DONE AFTER CAREFUL DELIBERATION AND FOR THE WELFARE OF MY SUBJECTS AND THE KINGDOM.

HE IS GOING TO PROCLAIM ME AS HIS SUCCESSOR.

I HAVE DECIDED TO WAIVE TRADITION...

...AND CROWN MY SON...

HE'S GOING TO ABDICATE IN MY FAVOUR!

... SAMUDRA GUPTA AS YOUR KING IN MY LIFETIME.

THEN HE WALKED UP TO SAMUDRA GUPTA AND EMBRACED HIM.

MY SON, MAY YOU RULE THE WHOLE WORLD!

ONLY KUMARADEVI NOTICED THE EFFECT CHANDRA GUPTA'S PROCLAMATION HAD ON KACHA.

LET ARRANGEMENTS BE MADE FOR THE CORONATION.

AND CHANDRA GUPTA MADE HIS EXIT,

The Glory of the Guptas

Script: Swarn Khandpur • Illustrations: Ramesh Umrotkar

THE RULE OF THE GUPTA DYNASTY (A.D. 320 TO 569) IS USUALLY KNOWN AS THE GOLDEN AGE OF INDIAN HISTORY. IT WAS A PERIOD OF PEACE AND PROSPERITY AND IT WITNESSED THE BLOSSOMING OF LITERATURE, SCIENCE AND THE ARTS.

IT WAS UNDER THE PATRONAGE OF THE GUPTA KINGS THAT SOME OF THE FINEST WORKS OF SANSKRIT POETRY AND DRAMA WERE WRITTEN. THE MOST FAMOUS POET AND DRAMATIST OF INDIA, KALIDASA, PROBABLY FLOURISHED DURING THIS TIME. HIS 'ABHIJNANA SHAKUNTALAM' IS WORLD-FAMOUS.

ARYABHATA, THE GREAT ASTRONOMER AND MATHEMATICIAN, WHO GAVE THE WORLD THE CONCEPT OF ZERO AND WHO WAS THE FIRST TO DISCOVER THAT THE EARTH REVOLVES ROUND THE SUN AND ROTATES ON ITS AXIS, TOO BELONGED TO THIS PERIOD.

THE IRON PILLAR AT DELHI, WHICH WEIGHS ABOUT 6 TONNES AND IS 7.32 METRES IN HEIGHT, IS A LIVING TRIBUTE TO THE GUPTA METALLURGISTS. DESPITE 2000 YEARS OF EXPOSURE TO WIND AND RAIN, IT DOES NOT HAVE EVEN A TRACE OF RUST!

ALTHOUGH MOST OF THE GUPTA KINGS WERE VAISHNAVAS, THEY WERE GENEROUS TO THE BUDDHISTS AND THE JAINS. THE AJANTA CAVES NEAR AURANGABAD WERE CARVED DURING THEIR REIGN. THE PAINTINGS ON THE WALLS, DEPICTING THE LIFE OF BUDDHA, HAVE SURVIVED TO THIS DAY.

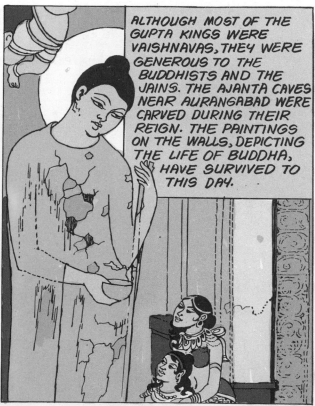

THERE WERE SEVERAL BUDDHIST MONASTERIES WHICH WERE AIDED BY ROYAL GRANTS. THE NALANDA MONASTERY, WHICH LATER BECAME A WORLD-FAMOUS UNIVERSITY, WAS FOUNDED DURING THE GUPTA PERIOD.

A COLLECTOR'S EDITION,
FROM INDIA'S FAVOURITE STORYTELLER.

India's greatest epic, told over 1,300 beautifully illustrated pages.
The Mahabharata Collector's Edition. It's not just a set of books, it's a piece of culture.

THE MAHABHARATA
COLLECTOR'S EDITION
Rupees one thousand, nine hundred and ninety-nine only.

LATER, WHEN THE COURTIERS WERE ALONE —

OUR KING TAKING A WIFE FROM THE LICHCHAVI OLIGARCHY IS ONE THING.

BUT MAKING A SON OF THAT UNION THE RULER IS QUITE ANOTHER. IT WAS AN UNWISE CHOICE.

ON THE CONTRARY, WITH HIM AS KING, WE CAN BE SURE OF THE CONTINUED POLITICAL AND MILITARY SUPPORT OF THE LICHCHAVIS.

THE COURTIER WHO SUPPORTED THE CHOICE WAS DHRUVABHUTI, CHIEF OF THE MILITARY AND HARISHENA'S FATHER.

WHAT IF HE ADOPTS THEIR HERETICAL CREEDS AND EN— DANGERS OUR OWN?

THE SON OF THE LICHCHAVI QUEEN SURPASSES ALL IN HIS GRASP OF THE ITIHASAS, THE DHARMA-SHASTRAS AND THE ARTHASHASTRA.

SO YOU CAN REST ASSURED THAT HIS RULE WILL BE GUIDED BY OUR TRADITIONAL VALUES.

THUS DID SAMUDRA GUPTA ASCEND THE THRONE EVEN IN THE LIFETIME OF HIS FATHER.

AFTER THE CORONATION —

MY QUEEN, AREN'T YOU HAPPY THAT YOUR SON IS THE RULER OF THE KINGDOM?

I AM AFRAID, MAHARAJ! AFRAID THAT KACHA'S DISAPPOINTMENT MIGHT MAKE HIM DO SOMETHING RASH...

... MIGHT TURN BROTHER AGAINST BROTHER... MIGHT DISTURB THE PEACE OUR KINGDOM HAS ENJOYED.

THEN I SHALL SET YOUR FEARS AT EASE, MY DEAR.

I AM CONFIDENT THAT SAMUDRA GUPTA CAN HANDLE ANY EVENTUALITY THAT MAY ARISE... IF IT DOES.

IT DID ARISE— SOONER THAN ANYONE COULD HAVE SUSPECTED.

MAHARAJ!

THERE IS TROUBLE AFOOT. KACHA HAS ISSUED COINS IN HIS NAME.

WHAT IS MORE, HE HAS SOUGHT THE SUPPORT OF THE NAGAS.

KACHA! MY BROTHER! TURNING TO THE NAGAS!

WHICH OF THEM?

ACHYUTSENA OF ROHILKHAND AND NAGASENA OF PADMAVATI. THE KING OF KOTA HAS JOINED THEM.

THEY ARE MARCHING TOWARDS THE CITY. KACHA HAS RIDDEN OUT TO MEET THEM.

AS THE OFFICIAL LEFT, HARISHENA BECAME THOUGHTFUL.

I HAVE HEARD FATHER SAY THAT THE NAGAS WERE NOT TOO HAPPY WITH THE POWER THE LICHCHAVI ALLIANCE GAVE US.

AND NOW THEY HOPE TO GET EVEN BY SUPPORTING FOOLISH KACHA! HMMM.

WELL, MAHARAJ! THE TIME HAS COME TO LAY DOWN THE LUTE...

...AND PICK UP THE BATTLE-AXE.

NO! NO! HARISHENA! KACHA IS MY BROTHER. I CANNOT...I WILL NOT RAISE WEAPONS AGAINST HIM!

YOU WILL, MAHARAJ.

REMEMBER KRISHNA'S ADVICE TO ARJUNA? REMEMBER YOUR ARGUMENT?

THE ONLY RELATIVE A KSHATRIYA HAS IS DHARMA.

22

YOU ARE FIRST A KING, AND THEN THE BROTHER OF KACHA.

AND HE MUST BE PREPARED TO FIGHT EVEN HIS OWN BROTHER IN DEFENCE OF DHARMA.

SAMUDRA GUPTA SLOWLY LOOKED UP AND SMILED AT HARISHENA.

THEN HE TOOK THE BATTLE-AXE FROM HIM...

...AND STOOD UP.

I SHALL NOT TOUCH THE LUTE TILL I HAVE NO MORE USE FOR THIS. ASK DHRUVABHUTI TO SEE ME.

SOON —

DHRUVABHUTI, RALLY OUR ARMIES. THE NAGAS MUST BE QUELLED.

AND SO SAMUDRA GUPTA, AT THE HEAD OF A VAST ARMY, MARCHED OUT WITH HARISHENA, HIS FAVOURITE AT COURT.

IN THE BATTLE THAT FOLLOWED EVEN HIS ENEMIES COULD NOT HELP BUT ADMIRE HIS PROWESS IN WAR.

WE HAVE NO HOPE, ACHYUTSENA.

THE FOOL, KACHA TOLD US THAT THE SON OF THE LICHCHAVI QUEEN COULD ONLY PLUCK THE STRINGS OF A LUTE.

THOSE ARMS COULD CONTAIN AN ELEPHANT, NAGASENA. KACHA HAS MADE FOOLS OF US!

WHERE IS KACHA?

WATCHING THE TURN THE BATTLE WAS TAKING, KACHA HAD FLED FROM THE SCENE AND WAS HEARD OF NO MORE.

SAMUDRA GUPTA WON THE BATTLE AND TOOK THE THREE KINGS CAPTIVE.

I AM SPARING YOUR LIVES. BUT LET THIS BE A LESSON TO YOU. NEVER PROVOKE ME AGAIN.

THEIR TERRITORIES WERE ANNEXED TO THE GUPTA KINGDOM.

AS SAMUDRA GUPTA RODE BACK TO THE CAPITAL —

HARISHENA, ONE THING SURPRISES ME. WITH ALL THE WISDOM OUR ANCIENTS HANDED DOWN TO US, WE STILL HAVE NOT BEEN ABLE TO HAVE UNITY IN OUR LAND.

THAT COULD COME ABOUT, AS THE ARTHA-SHASTRA TEACHES US, ONLY WITH ONE STRONG IMPERIAL AUTHORITY HOLDING SWAY OVER ALL THE PETTY STATES AND TRIBAL REPUBLICS.

THEN WE SHALL BECOME THAT AUTHORITY.

SO WHEN SAMUDRA GUPTA RETURNED TO THE CAPITAL —

MAHARAJ, SHALL I BRING OUT THE LUTE?

NO, DATTADEVI, THE TIME FOR THAT IS YET TO COME.

AH, DHRUVABHUTI! HAVE YOU DRAWN UP PLANS FOR THE CAMPAIGN?

CAMPAIGN?

YES, DEAR. I AM PLANNING TO TAKE OVER THE MADRAKA, YAUDHEYA, ARJUNAYANA, PRARJUNA, MALAVA, ABHIRA, SANAKANIKA, KAKA AND KHARAPARIKA REPUBLICS.

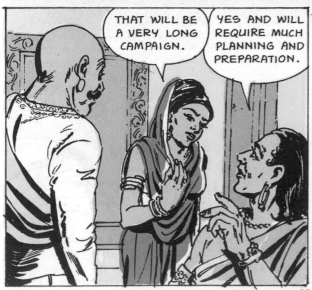

THAT WILL BE A VERY LONG CAMPAIGN.

YES AND WILL REQUIRE MUCH PLANNING AND PREPARATION.

THEN I SHALL NOT DISTURB YOU.

AND SO BEGAN THE MASSIVE OPERATIONS PREPARATORY TO A LONG CAMPAIGN.

MEANWHILE NEWS OF THE PREPARATIONS AND OF THE DEFEAT OF THE THREE KINGS SPREAD AND HAD A MOST UNEXPECTED RESULT. ONE DAY —

MAHARAJ, A REPRESENTATIVE OF THE YAUDHEYAS SEEKS AN AUDIENCE.

OH! I WILL SEE HIM AT COURT.

LATER —

OUR TRIBE OFFERS YOU TRIBUTE AS OUR MOST RESPECTED OVERLORD, AND SEEKS YOUR PROTECTION AND FRIENDSHIP AT ALL TIMES.

YOUR OFFER IS ACCEPTED IF YOU AGREE NOT TO WAGE WAR AMONG YOURSELVES OR WITH ANY OTHER WHO ENJOYS OUR PROTECTION.

AN OFFICIAL OF OUR COURT WILL BE PLACED IN YOUR REPUBLIC TO ENSURE PEACE AT ALL TIMES.

OVER THE NEXT FEW MONTHS, ONE BY ONE, EACH OF THE TRIBES CAME WITH THE SAME OFFER AND WAS GIVEN THE SAME REPLY. AND SO WITHOUT A STRUGGLE, WITHOUT ANY BLOODSHED, THE TRIBES BECAME FEUDAL STATES OF THE GROWING GUPTA POWER.

WHEN THE LAST OF THE REPRESENTATIVES HAD COME AND GONE —

WHAT DO WE DO WITH ALL THE MEN WE HAVE RALLIED... ALL THE WEAPONS... ALL THE EQUIPMENT?

NOTHING IS LOST. WE STILL GO ON OUR CAMPAIGN. BUT WE TAKE A DIFFERENT ROUTE.

WE GO SOUTHWARDS INSTEAD OF WESTWARDS.

?

HARISHENA SHOOK HIS HEAD AND SMILED TO HIMSELF.

WELL, MAHARAJ. I WILL NEVER UNDERSTAND YOU.

AND SO, BEGAN SAMUDRA GUPTA'S LONG MARCH SOUTHWARDS.

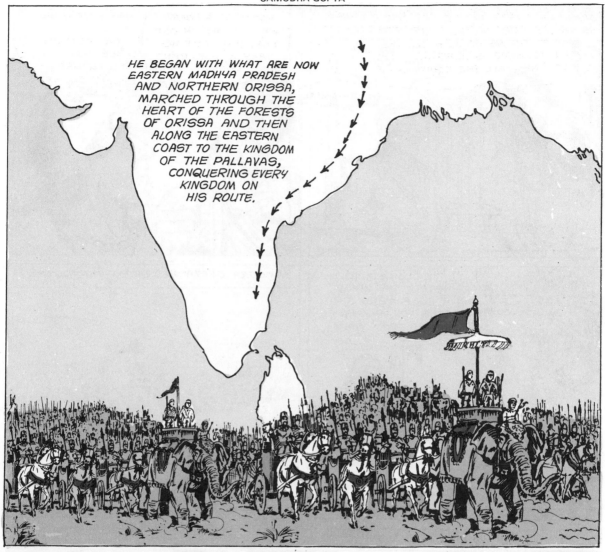

HE BEGAN WITH WHAT ARE NOW
EASTERN MADHYA PRADESH
AND NORTHERN ORISSA,
MARCHED THROUGH THE
HEART OF THE FORESTS
OF ORISSA AND THEN
ALONG THE EASTERN
COAST TO THE KINGDOM
OF THE PALLAVAS,
CONQUERING EVERY
KINGDOM ON
HIS ROUTE.

AS HE WAS PREPARING TO MARCH FURTHER SOUTH, NEWS CAME FROM THE NORTH.

MAHARAJ, ACHYUTSENA AND NAGASENA ARE PLANNING AN UPRISING. THEY HAVE ALLIED THEMSELVES WITH SIX OTHER NAGA RAJAS UNDER GANAPATINAGA OF MATHURA.

SAMUDRA GUPTA WAS QU'ET FOR A WHILE AS HE DID SOME QUICK REASONING. THEN —

HARISHENA. WE ARE TURNING BACK.

OUR CAMPAIGN WAS SUCCESSFUL. BUT STAYING BACK TO CONSOLIDATE OUR POSITION IS NOT POSSIBLE. NOT NOW, NOR IN THE FUTURE.

I HAVE DECIDED TO REINSTATE THE KINGS WITH ALL POWERS AND SETTLE FOR AN ANNUAL TRIBUTE FROM THEM.

SAMUDRA GUPTA RETRACED HIS ROUTE...

...SET THE KINGS BACK ON THEIR THRONES, ON HIS TERMS...

... AND AT LAST REACHED HIS CAPITAL TO MAKE PREPARATIONS FOR THE BATTLE AHEAD.

HARISHENA, I HAVE MADE UP MY MIND.

ABOUT WHAT NOW?

31

ON RETURNING TO HIS CAPITAL, HE PERFORMED THE ASHWAMEDHA SACRIFICE, TO WHICH KINGS FROM PARTS OF AFGHANISTAN, PERSIA, SRI LANKA AND SOUTH-EAST ASIA SENT THEIR ENVOYS WITH GIFTS.

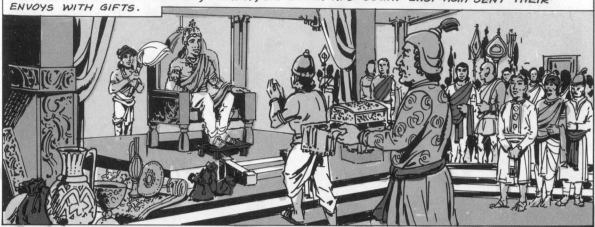

MEGHAVARNA, THE KING OF SRI LANKA, EVEN SOUGHT PERMISSION TO BUILD MONASTERIES FOR THE SRI LANKA BUDDHISTS IN SAMUDRA GUPTA'S EMPIRE. IT WAS READILY GRANTED.

WHEN ALL THE RITUALS AND FESTIVITIES CAME TO AN END —

MAHARAJ!

IN THE LAST TEN YEARS OF HIS REIGN, SAMUDRA GUPTA SAW HIS DREAM BECOME A REALITY. THE ORDER AND STABILITY HE HAD BROUGHT ABOUT, PAVED THE WAY FOR CHANDRA GUPTA II, HIS SON BORN OF DATTADEVI, TO CARRY THE GUPTA GLORY TO ITS ZENITH. LITERATURE AND THE ARTS FLOURISHED, EARNING THE GUPTA AGE THE EPITHET "GOLDEN".

HARSHA

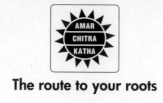

The route to your roots

HARSHA

Starting off as the ruler of tiny Thaneshwar, Harsha (7th century AD) rose to become the powerful monarch of the kingdom of Kanauj. He avenged the wicked assassination of his elder brother and the cowardly abduction of his sister. His biographer Bana Bhatta and the Chinese traveller Hiuen Tsang were unanimous in their praise of this learned king, whose fame did much to create a glowing image of India in lands far away.

Script
Yagya Sharma
Anand Prakash Singh

Illustrations
Madhu Powle

Editor
Anant Pai

ABOUT 1,400 YEARS AGO, THANESHWAR, A POWERFUL KINGDOM IN NORTHERN INDIA WAS RULED BY PRABHAKAR VARDHAN. DURING THIS PERIOD THE HUNS HAD STARTED HARASSING THE PEOPLE OF THANESHWAR. SO THE KING SENT HIS ABLE SONS TO PUNISH THEM.

AFTER A BITTER FIGHT, THE HUNS RETREATED:

VICTORY TO PRINCE RAJYAVARDHAN! VICTORY TO PRINCE HARSHA!

HALT! IT IS GETTING DARK. LET US STOP FOLLOWING THEM.

YES, BROTHER! LET US CAMP HERE.

THE HUNS DID NOT ATTACK AGAIN.

THERE HAS BEEN NO FIGHTING FOR SEVERAL DAYS. I THINK I'LL GO ON A HUNT.

ALL RIGHT, HARSHA!

THE TIME IS RIPE. WE CAN NOW GRAB THE KINGDOMS OF THANESHWAR AND KANNAUJ.

BUT THEY ARE VERY POWERFUL, SIR.

I KNOW. BUT IF WE KILL GRAHAVARMAN, THE INEXPERIENCED RAJYAVARDHAN WILL NOT BE ABLE TO DEFEND BOTH KINGDOMS.

BUT HOW ARE WE GOING TO KILL GRAHAVARMAN?

I HAVE A PLAN. DURING THE SPRING FESTIVAL, WE WILL DISGUISE OURSELVES AS SIMPLE PEASANTS AND MINGLE WITH THE COMMONERS OF KANNAUJ. WHEN GRAHAVARMAN COMES TO CELEBRATE THE FESTIVAL WITH HIS PEOPLE, WE WILL KILL HIM.

ACCORDING TO THEIR PLAN, DEVGUPTA AND HIS SOLDIERS DRESSED IN ORDINARY CLOTHES, MINGLED WITH THE PEOPLE OF KANNAUJ. THEN AS KING GRAHAVARMAN WAS ENTERING A TEMPLE —

MAHARAJ, ALLOW ME TO ATTACK MALWA.

NO, HARSHA!

BEING THE ELDER BROTHER AND THE KING IT IS MY DUTY TO DO SO.

YOU HAVE BEHAVED LIKE A COWARD.

MEANWHILE IN MALWA—

SAY WHATEVER YOU LIKE. BUT I SHALL SOON BE THE KING OF KANNAUJ AS WELL AS THANESHWAR.

IMPRISON HER. LET HER LEARN TO RESPECT A KING.

THE SIGHTS IN THE PRISON DISTURBED RAJYASHRI.

THE PAINFUL CRIES OF OTHER PRISONERS AGONISED HER HEART AND SOUL.

OH, MY GOD!

WHILE RAJYASHRI WAS SUFFERING MENTALLY, DEVGUPTA WAS ENJOYING HIMSELF.

JUST THEN DEVGUPTA RECEIVED A MESSAGE.

RAJYAVARDHAN IS PREPARING TO ATTACK US, SIR!

I EXPECTED THIS. GO AND CALL KING SHASHANK OF GAUD. I WANT TO TALK TO HIM.

VERY SOON DEVGUPTA WAS SCHEMING WITH SHASHANK.

I WILL SHARE HALF OF THE KINGDOMS OF THANE-SHWAR AND KANNAUJ WITH YOU IF YOU HELP ME.

I WILL. WHAT MUST I DO?

WIN RAJYAVARDHAN'S CONFIDENCE AND ACCOMPANY HIM IN HIS ATTACK ON ME.

WHEN THE BATTLE BEGINS, ATTACK RAJYAVARDHAN FROM THE REAR. ONCE HE IS DEAD, WE'VE AS GOOD AS WON.

YOUR PLAN IS EXCELLENT. WE SHALL DEFINITELY SUCCEED.

THUS RAJYASHRI ESCAPED FROM DEVGUPTA'S PRISON.

DEVGUPTA'S SOLDIERS WERE PATROLLING THE JUNGLE, BUT LUCKILY SHE WAS NOT SPOTTED BY THEM.

FINALLY RAJYASHRI ESCAPED INTO THE JUNGLE.

MEANWHILE RAJYAVARDHAN FOUGHT FIERCELY. SHASHANK WAS HELPLESS AS HE WAS SURROUNDED BY RAJYAVARDHAN'S PERSONAL GUARDS.

FINALLY RAJYAVARDHAN KILLED DEVGUPTA AND WON THE BATTLE.

VICTORY TO MAHARAJ RAJYA-VARDHAN.

SHASHANK WAS VERY UPSET OVER THE DEATH OF DEVGUPTA.

WITH DEV-GUPTA'S DEATH, MY DREAMS ARE ALSO SHATTERED.

BUT IF I SOMEHOW KILL RAJYAVARDHAN, HIS KINGDOM WILL BECOME WEAK AND THEN I SHALL GRAB IT EASILY.

NOW WE SHOULD MAKE PLANS FOR THE FUTURE. PLEASE COME TO MY TENT TONIGHT.

I WILL COME.

THAT NIGHT IN SHASHANK'S TENT —

NOW I MUST ESCAPE IMMEDIATELY.

HARSHA WAS RETURNING HOME AFTER CONQUERING KATHIAWAR. HIS SOLDIERS WERE TIRED AND EAGER TO REACH HOME.

AND AT THAT MOMENT PULAKESHIN ATTACKED HARSHA.

THE FIGHTING CONTINUED FOR SEVERAL DAYS.
LOSSES WERE HEAVY ON BOTH SIDES.

HARSHA'S TIRED SOLDIERS HAD TO
RETREAT. HE WAS VERY SAD.

ALL THOSE MEN WERE KILLED FOR NOTHING.

SOMETIME LATER IN THANESHWAR—

MAHARAJ HARSHA, LET US ATTACK PULAKESHIN. THIS TIME WE ARE FULLY PREPARED TO CRUSH HIM.

I HAVE HAD ENOUGH OF THIS BLOOD-SHED.

TO FULFIL HIS DREAM, HARSHA GAVE FINANCIAL HELP TO THE POOR.

HE APPOINTED PHYSICIANS TO TREAT THE SICK FREE OF COST.

HE HELPED STUDENTS TO PURSUE THEIR STUDIES.

DURING HIS TIME, TRADERS CAME FROM AS FAR AS CHINA.

PEOPLE PROSPERED.

AND FOLLOWERS OF DIFFERENT FAITHS LIVED IN PEACE AND HARMONY.

DURING THIS PERIOD, HIUEN TSANG, THE FAMOUS CHINESE PILGRIM AND SCHOLAR CAME TO INDIA. AFTER SPENDING SOME TIME IN EASTERN INDIA, HE MET HARSHA.

MAHARAJ, A BUDDHIST MONK WANTS TO SEE YOU.

BRING HIM IN.

WELCOME, SCHOLAR HIUEN TSANG. I WAS LOOKING FORWARD TO MEETING YOU.

MAHARAJ, I AM HONOURED.

SIR, I HAVE COME HERE TO LEARN MORE ABOUT THE BUDDHIST RELIGION.

I HOPE, YOU FIND YOUR STAY COMFORTABLE

HIUEN TSANG STAYED IN INDIA FOR A FEW YEARS.

DURING HIUEN TSANG'S STAY, HARSHA DECIDED TO HOLD A SEMINAR ON RELIGIONS.

MINISTER, PLEASE INVITE SCHOLARS OF DIFFERENT RELIGIONS TO TAKE PART IN THIS SEMINAR.

EMINENT SCHOLARS OF HINDUISM, JAINISM AND BUDDHISM CAME TO PARTICIPATE IN THE SEMINAR.

THE SEMINAR CONTINUED FOR SEVERAL DAYS.

HIUEN TSANG TOO PARTICIPATED IN THE SEMINAR.

ACHARYA HIUEN TSANG, YOU ARE THE MOST NOBLE SCHOLAR I HAVE EVER KNOWN.

BUT SOME OF THE GREEDY PARTICIPANTS DID NOT LIKE THAT A FOREIGNER SHOULD BE PRAISED BY THIER KING.

IF HIUEN TSANG MAKES A GOOD IMPRESSION ON THE KING, WE MAY NOT GET THOSE RICH REWARDS, WE EXPECT.

YES, HE MUST BE FINISHED BEFORE HE DOES MORE HARM.

BUT THIS CONSPIRACY WAS REPORTED TO HARSHA IMMEDIATELY.

I WARN THE CONSPIRATORS THAT ANYBODY WHO TRIES TO HARM ACHARYA HIUEN TSANG SHALL BE PUNISHED. PROCLAIM THIS TO ALL.

I BELIEVE IN NON-VIOLENCE, THE POOR AND THE WEAK SHALL BE PROTECTED. THOSE WHO PREACH VIOLENCE SHALL PAY FOR IT WITH THEIR OWN LIVES.

AS A RESULT OF THIS STERN WARNING, NOBODY TRIED TO HARM HIUEN TSANG.

THE SEMINAR IS OVER. THE SCHOLARS SHOULD NOW BE PRESENTED WITH GIFTS.

THE ARRANGEMENTS HAVE BEEN MADE, MAHARAJ!

FROM THE NEXT DAY, HARSHA STARTED PRESENTING GIFTS TO THE SCHOLARS AND PRIESTS OF DIFFERENT RELIGIONS.

THEN CAME THE TURN OF POOR PEASANTS.

SOON THE GIFTS BROUGHT FOR DONATION WERE EXHAUSTED. BUT STILL MANY PEOPLE REMAINED WITHOUT GIFTS.

BRING ALL THE REMAINING WEALTH FROM THE ROYAL TREASURY.

AS YOU WISH, MAHARAJ.

THE ROYAL WEALTH WAS ALSO GIVEN AWAY BUT EVEN THEN SOME PEOPLE WERE LEFT OUT.

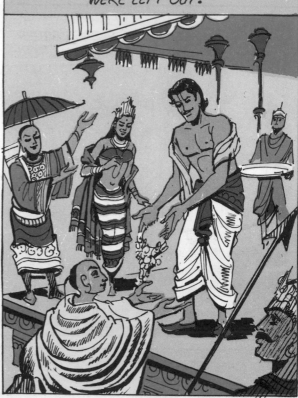

HERE TAKE MY ORNAMENTS. OF WHAT USE ARE THEY IF MY PEOPLE LIVE IN MISERY.

IN THE END ONLY ONE MAN WAS LEFT OUT.

I AM SORRY THAT NOTHING IS LEFT WITH ME EXCEPT THE CLOTHES I AM WEARING. PLEASE ACCEPT THEM.

In this manner, every five years, Harsha gave away all his wealth to the scholars, the priests and the poor.